Girl **Talk**

Nancy McCleery

The Backwaters Press
Omaha

ACKNOWLEDGMENTS

Thanks to the following publications where some of these poems first appeared, occasionally in earlier versions:

Café Solo; *Forty Nebraska Poets*; *In the Dreamland, Alaskan Writers*; *Inroads, Alaska's Fellowships Winners*; *Kansas Quarterly*; *Many Mountains Moving*; *Many Voices, One Song*; NEW.; *Pebble*; *Periodical of Art in Nebraska*; *Plains Songs Review*; *Poetry and Prose International Anthology*; *Saltillo*; *Silver Vain*; *Times of Sorrow, Times of Grace*; *Whole Notes*; and *Writers Forum*.

Two of the poems also appeared on broadside from bradypress and Sandhills Press; others in mixed-media installations: *Runes and Ruins* with video, in collaboration with visual artist David Edlefsen and with dancers, Visual Arts Center, Anchorage, Alaska, November 1987; *Women, Fire and Dangerous Things,* by visual artist Nancy Childs, Lincoln, Nebraska, Summer 1993; and *Girl Talk,* produced by Judy Hart, actor, and Nancy Marshall, musician, Lincoln, Nebraska, March 1995.

Five of the poems were included earlier in *Staying the Winter,* The Cummington Press, 1987; two poems appeared in *Polar Lights,* Transient Press, 1994; and twelve poems were presented in *Blown Roses,* a limited edition chapbook from bradypress, 2001.

Particular thanks for their encouragement and interest to the many poets, printers, artists, musicians and writers in my life, to my family, my friends, and many others who helped along the way.

I also thank the Alaska State Council on the Arts for Travel Grants in 1978, 1982, and 1987 and for Individual Artist Fellowships in Literature in 1980 and 1986. Thanks also to the Nebraska Arts Council for an Individual Artist Fellowship in 1995, all of which provided time to complete a number of these poems.

Copyright © 2002 by Nancy McCleery

No part of this collection may be reproduced in any form whatsoever, except for brief quotations in reviews, without the express written permission of the author or publisher.

Backwaters Press logo designed by L. L. Mannlein

Copyright © The Backwaters Press 1997

Greg Kosmicki, Editor and Publisher

3502 North 32 St, Omaha NE 68104-3506 / (402) 451-4052

GKosm62735@aol.com

www.thebackwaterspress.homestead.com

ISBN 0-9677149-9-0

Printed in the USA by Morris Publishing

CONTENTS

1 The Burden of the Valley of Vision

   Girl Talk (litany) 3
   Girl Talk (AIDS / quilt) 5
   Girl Talk (m. ernst) 7
   Girl Talk (give / hold) 9
   Girl Talk (philosophy) 10
   Girl Talk (v. monologues) 12
   Girl Talk (break of day) 13
   Girl Talk (beautiful / smiles / 1968) 14
   Girl Talk (coffee / china) 15
      Incense 16
      The Word 17
      Another Day in Paradise 18
      It's March 19

2 Some of the Best Friends

      Windows 23
   Girl Talk (family) 24
      Flowers, Glass, Stars, and River 26
   Girl Talk (memorial) 27
      Long Distance Conversations 29
      My Daughter Brings Me Garbage Flowers 30
   Girl Talk (cereus) 31
      To My Small Daughter 32
      My Son Brings Bagpipe Music 33
      Sunday Afternoons My Son Bakes Bread 34
      To My Small Son 35
      Last Night Dreaming and in the Dream Barbara
         Shows Me Her New Poem 36
      Magic Slim on the Radio 37
      A Window 38
      The Siamese Cat Is Sleeping 39
      Bird Song 40
      From Weeping Water 41
      The Four-Quartered Universe 42
      By the *Kits-ka-toos* (the Platte) 43

    View of Pawnee Origins   44
    By the Nelchina   45
    Fragments Concerning the Canopic Jars   46
    Girl Talk (paper)   47
        1 AM poem   48
        Friends, These Gifts   49

3 Love / Work / Travel

    Girl Talk (aristotle)   53
    Girl Talk (light)   54
    Girl Talk (room / for writing)   55
    Girl Talk (trash)   58
    Girl Talk (tracings)   59
        Card Player   60
    Girl Talk (The Standing-in-Blue-Flags Painting)   61
    Girl Talk (Another-Little-Love-Poem Painting)   62
    Girl Talk (poetry / reading)   63
    Girl Talk (heart / meditation)   65
    Girl Talk (bosh / save)   66
    Girl Talk (leaving)   67
        Why   69
    Girl Talk (nine / 9)   70
        Christmas Letter from Alaska   71
        December Notes   72
        Juan de Fuca, Port Townsend   73
        Wright's Beach, Northern California   74
        Hands   75

4 Space

    Girl Talk (negative / space)   79
    Girl Talk (lists)   81
    Girl Talk (music / purity)   82
    Girl Talk (lazy / domestic)   83
        What We're Doing, First
                and Foremost   84
    Girl Talk (high / bird)   85
    Girl Talk (after images)   86

Girl Talk (Dream-and-Love-Collage-with-Text)   87
Girl Talk (dream lines / frescoes)   88
   Lines before Sleep   89
   Flowers and Friends   90
   In David City Park   92
Girl Talk (sky / sleep)   93
Girl Talk (*reflets dans l'eau* / debussy / reflections)   94

5 Lingo

Girl Talk (piano)   97
Girl Talk (brain / dump)   98
    The Mailman   99
Girl Talk (crab)   100
Girl Talk (night bird)   101
Girl Talk (frames)   102
   Sleep Talk   103
Girl Talk (dream / call)   104
   Love Poem   105
Girl Talk (passion / mind)   106
Girl Talk (super h'way)   107
Girl Talk (difficult)   108
Girl Talk (letter / love)   109
Girl Talk (monarchs)   110
Girl Talk (eternity)   111
Girl Talk (subtexts)   113
   Department Store Visit   114
   On Receiving a Postcard from St. Tropez   116
Girl Talk (trail / horses)   117
Girl Talk (lingo)   118
Girl Talk (buddha)   119
Girl Talk (the book / Job)   120

6 On Holy Ground

   Night Summons   123
Girl Talk (her art)   124
   Waiting for the Last Angel   125
Girl Talk (AIDS project / names)   126

    Return   128
    Percival's Final Questions   129
    The Tribe   130
    Angel of the Hollow Hills   131
    Lullabye   132
Girl Talk (angels)   133
    The Visitor   135
    When It Is Over   136
    Love: The Red, Red Rose?   137
    Let It Happen   138
    No Matter How Lost   139
    Girl Talk (every day / every night / walking out)   140
Girl Talk (winning / losing)   141

For Robin and David, my family and my friends

*in memory of my parents
David Ransom Hill and Esther Koch Hill*

*and dedicated to all the victims
of HIV/AIDS, particularly John Goldring, 1943-1987,
Anchorage, Alaska, award-winning director and playwright.
May the awareness and memory continue.
May our work and friendships thrive.*

1 The Burden of the Valley of Vision

... If there's room for poets in this world ...
Their sole work ... represent the age,
Their age ... this live throbbing age,
That brawls, cheats, maddens, calculates, aspires,
And spends more passions, more heroic heat....

Never flinch.

from "Aurora Leigh," Elizabeth Barrett Browning, 1857

A poetry ...
that, from literal or imagined experience, depicts
and denounces perennial injustice and cruelty
in their current forms and in our peculiar time warns
of the unprecedented perils that confront us,
[also] ... can be truly poetry.

Denise Levertov, early 1980s

Girl Talk (litany)

Told me the only way she could get to sleep
was to recite the names of all the lovers
she'd ever had. Like a litany. Told me
so often I thought they were mine, at least
a couple of them. So many you'd think
it was the countdown for a blastoff
but it didn't excite her, it nearly put her
to sleep there at lunch. She'd start off with Neil
in the back seat of his beat-up Toyota
and end up dozing with Darrell in the weeds
behind the barn, not to forget Shaun
underneath the awnings of the Country Club Lounge
or maybe in the shower at the Hilton. Or Horace
at the beach. Steve on the stove swear to God.
Rod while he carried her up the stairs and in every room
in the house, how she'd sneak in some John's office
or home when the boss or the wife were gone.
Ron was easy. Any place. Any time.
She didn't exactly explain and I couldn't
really tell from the tone in her voice, the look
on her face, whether she was complaining or bragging.
Probably neither. If she was to be believed,
it was if she didn't count them she'd end up
with visions of Fred, her good buddy and never
a lover, Fred who died of AIDS last year,
so she'd keep the roll call going past
Fred to a tap dancer who had to shoot up
insulin beforehand on account of he had diabetes,
all the way to George who always checked first
to make sure she didn't have any warts on her hands,
but she'd somehow get back to the sweet
and gentle ones with names like Kent
or Ryan. She'd tell me all this at lunch
and I'd think her face would probably fall
in her soup at any time. Sure, she'd yawn

whatever else they wanna eat—
Instant Party! but best those times
he'd look long and hard at my canvases
sorta' walk into 'em without sayin' a word
just absorbin' 'em 'n on the way out a hug
'n thanks imagine thanks for just lookin'
many silent minutes at my work.

                               She paused

Never have a friend like Fred, she mumbled,
like the old Joni Mitchell song says
ya don't know whatcha got till it's gone
the town changed 'n he'd've moved on
just like me so anyway here I am.

Her voice trailed off so I barely heard her.
She went back to painting on a quilt panel.
For him.

                    Given a little privacy, I'd have cried.

Girl Talk (m. ernst)

Told me she wasn't sure what her vision was,
what it focused on or amounted to.

And she said, Max Ernst wrote something
about being able to see his vision
recognizing it but never teaching it any words

once you say the words they start to slip
'n are all but gone when all said they *are* gone

your poetry's made of nothin' but pencil scratches
'n breath just a little more layin' on of the hands
we could lay out your text on my work or
you could work your fingers on your piano

but the song wafts away like the poem
one stroke one word at a time.

In a non sequitur, she continued,
maybe that's why hand-minded visual artists
are better cooks better lovers
than most word-minded writers.

Told her I was not ready to concede that,
not ready to rally my evidence to the contrary,
not ready to debate it at all, but
I respected the Ernst quote and when she
found it, exactly word for word,
I'd take it down, lift it up with new words.

Or better. I'd present you with the uncarved block.

Yes, she told me, what she was after, after all, was
what vanishes, best of all, the repeating dream.

She saw the hawk and she *was* the hawk,
riding a thermal up and around,
circling despite her fear of letting
rising winds take her away,

over the mountains to the seashore and
beyond, ever higher on spiraling currents,
until only a speck of herself remained.

She told me when she awakened,
it was orgasmic where she'd been,

what she'd been up to.

Girl Talk (give / hold)

Told me there's her work, she can hold it
in her hands, observe it and it suffices,

while the guitarist, she declared, holds a note
then gives it away like reading poetry aloud
you hold the silence then feel it in your mind
give it breath and let it go

so *let's* go, she suddenly insisted,
to the Zoo Bar let's find Magic Slim
and the Teardrops back from the Netherlands
since we don't grieve so much anymore
we'll let the music do it for us
get t' feelin' good about feelin' bad

let's go hear the blues they never die.

She was out the door dancing
and humming "Ride, Sally, Ride."

Girl Talk (philosophy)

She was humming "Amazing Grace," then stopped.
Looking at me hard and long, she took a deep breath.

Told me she called the cops when the neighbor
got slung against the floor and the wall
but the woman let her man back into the apartment.
And, she said, to make a point I called
the woman "Nicole" to her face it seemed
to go over her head she didn't get it.

Singing, she changed the subject
   "*Row, row, row your boat*
   Gently down the stream.
   La   l'La   l'La   l'La
   Life is   but   a dream."
On the heels of that, she recited
   "*Sit on a cushion and sew a fine seam.*
   Feed upon strawberries sugar and cream."
She continued: since I was a child
they've sounded just right to me
helped my art my own little candle
lit wherever I am enough cash
for art supplies some Soave wine
dinner out goin' t' hear the Blues
lettin' the rest of the world go by
til I learn a friend has breast cancer or
a widow too frail to drive can't get
out of town not even a day trip
so I drive run errands take a casserole

but the world, she continued, Belfast
Beirut Bosnia Johannesburg Jerusalem
religion 'n race in the US in Tibet
in Uganda and everywhere AIDS unwanted
pregnancies homeless hungry uninsured

the poor we always have with us
how long o lord, how long?

The world, I interjected, too much with us,
clarification after we stir things up.

Yes, she said, Amnesty International
Southern Poverty Law Center NOW
a woman for Congress for Senate for President
next time my check with yours to Amnesty
and others let's pool our money.

Later, I said, contemplating her latest collage,
the impenetrable written text. Her visual
language: some dried flower petals,
vintage lace, old bus tickets, photos.

Then she began humming again: "*If I had a hammer.*"
And in a non sequitur, told me:
Ya' know lots 'a folks think I'm a hard-ass
egotist whiner whore a woose dreamer
neurotic paranoid totally right-brained . . .

Because I'm her friend, I whispered, My Dear,
do you ever think before you speak?

Without missing a beat, she looked me
dead in the eye: Rarely   if I did
I'd probably never say anything at all.
    Her last words to me that day.

I thought without saying, how like each of us:
    a crystal held up to the light,
one facet alone catching the most of it.

And I looked
    to be surprised.

Girl Talk (v. monologues)

Told me about a girlfriend of hers, an artist:

> as a child abused head t' toe 'n in between
> inside out 'n she's never seen a counselor
>
> but she's workin' with imagery of clenched fists
> also of Georgia O'Keefe-like flowers
>
> could be like Tennessee Williams' definition:
> a bruised orchid his vagina metaphor
>
> but if she sees Sarandon Oprah Whoopie
> 'n others in Ensler's *The Vagina Monologues*
> maybe it'll help get rid of what plagues her
>
> since we'll be in New York City soon
> for a retrospective of art at the Whitney
> I bought tickets for us for that show.

I asked her to take good notes for me
and right on key, once she'd had her say,

she focused on her work, another AIDS piece,
a collage. Didn't say who it was for.

Girl Talk (break of day)

Told me bare-chested good looks
wearing gold-rimmed designer sunglasses
clean chino cutoffs Italian sandals
the young man below my bedroom window
tan smooth California blonde

hoists a fifty-gallon orange plastic
barrel spills in my trash 'n dumps it

into the back of the truck 'n then
comes again to the row of garbage cans

lifts from one a kerosene lamp
takes it to the cab 'n says not bad

then over the truck's idlin' engine
he calls to his workin' buddy:

> I'd just like to say to someone
> who says oh yer just a garbage man:
>
>> Yeah 'n I got a degree in psychology
>> 'n one in architecture so what about
>> the fuckin' government 'n its socio-
>> economic strategies Smart Ass

She told me: truth stranger than ya know what.

Girl Talk (beautiful / smiles / 1968)

Told me: I'll tell you about the beautiful
red-haired woman in the turquoise raincoat

on foot so to speak just south
of the old Brandeis buildin' at 10th and N
her coat open flappin' in the drizzly breeze
her dress knee length flowing pale pink

on crutches with hair blowin' back
from her face a slight smile

gimpin' along on her left foot her right leg
only as long as one of her arms maybe shorter
this leg swingin' back 'n forth
with a tiny shoe on that tiny foot

the leg just flappin' 'n her smilin'
makin' good time on only one high heel
sling pumps black patent leather

she needed those crutches she needed more
than that 'n maybe she's found it

she was goin' toward a tall fella
he was startin' to walk her direction
he'd been waitin' for her I think

the man I was with looked twice
    cuz, he said, she was beautiful she
    looked angelic her porcelain face
    they *both* looked beatific saintlike

    her head circled with a halo of light.

Girl Talk (coffee / china)

Told me handpicked by Juan Valdez 'n
yes Colombian coffee gets the morning
out of bed 'n into the springtime shower
puts me safe on the streets with a full belly
all this good life paradise stuff
but can't help seeing Juan moonlightin'
in coke fields his wife 'n kids not knowin'
how famous on TV his name his fingers

'n there's this woman at her knittin' machine
somewhere in China puttin' together 'n
on my very back this white cotton sweater
wonderin' what she'd be
had she been so lucky
t've been made in the USA.

1994

Incense

Suspended from the eaves, the birdfeeder
banged all day against the clapboard siding.
One quiet moment at dusk, the air fresh from
snow newly fallen, cardinals, bluejays, and
chickadees fought each other for a feeding place.

Inside, a pungent fragrance, faint smoke
filling the house. How easily the match was
struck. Now frankincense. Now myrrh.

Nightfall. On PBS the Soviets and Azerbaijanis
gathering in rebellion, the film producer foregoing
a new car, buys hundreds of video tapes instead,
sends copies around the world. Even
Gorbachev has one. On a Mediterranean hillside,
a shepherd gathers his sheep. A priest
surveys ruined icons, lights a censer,
the ritual of incense. Who and where
are the sparrows? Where in God's eye are they:

>The rag lady on Zero Street?
>The single mother in the welfare line?
>The first case of AIDS on the block?
>The women, children and men of Lithuania,
>in Israel, in Turkey, in Kuwait, in Iraq?
>And where, the Armenians?
>Etc.   Etc.   Etc.   Etc.

And so it continues. Incense, wafted away.
Earlier a slight breeze settled down
around the house. Turn off TV,
get some rest. But just now,
a loud wind rises.

1991

The Word

has its own sound.
Say it is like a man
or woman returning to us
from war who calls out,
    "I am here."

And we all feel safe
for an instant.
Then for a time
we hear the echo.

Making it a gift
to ourselves
and to each other,
we celebrate.

Another day comes
and we miss it.

But the word is out.
Say it.
We may know it
when we hear it.

Another Day in Paradise

> *Then the moon shall be confounded,*
> *and the sun ashamed.*
> Isaiah 24:23

I lay my hand down on the brow of the woman
for whom this gesture means incest, rape, battering.

I lay my hand down on the basket of berries
grown by the river. I give the river,
the salmon back to the berry picker.

I lay my pen down for the first song. I lay
my forearms down on the kitchen table
for all peacemakers. I lay my head down

for the homeless, the war veterans, the victims,
of AIDS, the dreams of America,
a nation failing and failed. I lay my body down
to a sleep of unrest, my dreams down in a thicket
of dry brambles ready for the fire.

The burden of the valley of vision.
The burden of the desert of the sea.

It's March

There are flowers
and other music

in places
where nothing

consoles
the wind

2 Some of the Best of Friends

A fish cannot drown in water,
    A bird does not fall in air ...
Each creature God made
    Must live in its own true nature. ...

        Mechtild of Magdeburg, 13th century

Windows

Moon at the top of the trees
        Roof of the house
All cloud-covered
        Barely discernible
An unnamed longing for
        Home

Girl Talk (family)

Told me *plus ça change plus la même chose*,
that she was both participant and survivor
of the *me generation* in the 1970s
when so many marriages split up.

Told me now twenty years later
grandkids drivin' to college 'n busy
with friends 'n most of my friends
into the rat race computer e-mail life
or traveling away on holidays, she said,

I go to my studio make art see a movie
volunteer at school help serve a meal
to the homeless which I number myself among
figuratively, she said, while I think I want
an old-fashioned turkey day xmas 4th of July
family round the old photo album
doin' dishes together takin' a ride
in the countryside but the flood carries life
downstream away never the same river twice
the new dreams the gone dreams prepare me
for that last white light my last *adios*
with no *sayanoras* no *alohas* no social
life there that I know of either.

Someday, great grandkids to care for, I said.

Maybe, she countered, but tonight it's watch
The Tango Lesson on video
Sally Potter 'n dancer Pablo Vernon
or tangle-tango with hot-blooded men.

Again she talked me into going dancing
looking for younger male dance partners.

For now, I admitted, yes, for now.

Then we're gone, she said, gone. And we were,

to the Fly-by-Night Bar and Starlight Ballroom
where I watched, she danced. I went home early.

Flowers, Glass, Stars, and River

The Colorado red stone carriage block at curb side,
    my grandparents' names, the year 1903
imbedded in the cement slab walking path

    alongside the large perennial flower garden,
two grape arbors, an eight-foot honeysuckle,
    the walnut, apple and cherry trees, and a widow

none of us know living now in the old Victorian house,
    the house in our family for a hundred years.
Mother—thirteen years gone from your heirloom garden,
    save for trumpet vine, coral bell, blue phlox,

resurrection lily, baby's breath, windflower in bloom—
    after your death we brought your iris bulbs
a hundred miles east to my daughter's garden, and

    to my garden: your seeds, your mother vine.
Your last summer Dad, in shade from the tree
    of paradise, across a card table set up

on the brick patio you had laid, you fashioned
    stained glass figures long before the fad,
your colors, reflecting more than my life—

    black circus seal, blue whale, brown thrush.
I see us wading in the cold again, building
    new channels in the dark, shallow waters,

the sandbars of the Platte. Some night,
    in a split second, I'll follow you both
into the white light, the ashes of these bones

    made of stars, scattered there
by my son, my daughter, my granddaughters.
    In the wind. In the river.

Girl Talk (memorial)

Told me she didn't go to Memorial Services
on International AIDS Day in December.
She explained: prayers litanies folks
recitin' names of those who've died
music pullin' my emotions 'n me
catchin' my breath to keep from cryin'

had a friend say when you cry and can't
control it or when it comes unexpectedly
as an overnight early autumn hard freeze
it means you're close to the sacred
that's sacred with a capital letter "s"
just don't want others to witness my breakdown
never did in front of Fred not once
not when he'd lost most of his hair
gaunt hollow-eyed as a holocaust survivor.

Yes, I responded, why the King Lear mode,
break down the border between the private
and the public self.

                          Told me she nearly did
a decade ago over a deluge of losses
most folks considered it gauche, she said,
politically incorrect immature in bad taste
then I bit the proverbial bullet went away
to my studio so now have my art work
'n memorials I need to call Fred's sister
soon as a new moon comes bringin' me courage

Fred's not on any list of AIDS victims
families tried to hide it in those days
is why there's no quilt panel for him

but on a June day in '87 his sister
sent his ashes sailin' over Big Sur
in one brief memorial so sorry

I couldn't get there for takin' care
of my mom in the Midwest miles away
her heart givin' out you'd've liked her
Fred too great spirits comin' from them
even now twelve years after their deaths.

Long Distance Conversations
for my son and my daughter

When I am gone he will walk alone
in the shallow Platte with a vial of my ashes.
He will crack the glass. He has promised.
My fifty-first Spring and I sweep dust
from the porch onto the leaf-cluttered lawn.

*

She and my granddaughter take long walks,
name the birds, the first flowers.
My ashes fall into the river.
We do not speak of these things with her.
She is teaching her daughter to sing.

My Daughter Brings Me Garbage Flowers,

digs them out of the floral shop
trash at the end of her work day,
an evening job arranging flowers,
lifting her spirits after teaching
Special Education. Blown roses,
mostly. Last week thirteen of them.
I don't stop smiling for days.
Deep red. Last month three lavender.
Sometimes pale yellow, pink, white.

Occasionally a mixed bouquet,
spring flowers. Flowers that don't
and won't sell. Too fully opened.
Wilting a bit. Old. Older.
We cherish, we salvage what we can.
Mirrors, these companions. Old friends.

Most want the virgin rose buds.
She knows I prefer the blatant,
immodest, blowzy, open blossoms.
Brings them wrapped in pastel tissue papers
holding them in her arms the way
I carried her before she walked.

Memorial Day week, the shop floor
covered with buckets of blue and white
hydrangeas, blue flags, freesias, carnations,
pots of green and yellow philodendron,
geraniums, petunias, lobelia. And peonies,
the beauty of pink and white and fuchsia
blooms. A backdrop for dreams in color.
Pale, still bodies of war dead. These tributes.

And there behind the counter, a knife
in her right hand, my daughter,
cutting thorns from stems. Smiling.

Girl Talk (cereus)
for Cara and Cal
9/11/2001

Outrageous flowers burst red and gold. New York City, mid-morning,
planes have flown into the World Trade Center's Twin Towers.
And into the Pentagon, into Pennsylvania earth.

Late morning, my friend Cara called: it could happen
tonight in their garden:
the night-blooming cereus—blooming only once a year.

While the plant gathers her energies,
we relate the horrors:
people and buildings falling in on themselves.

Now, in the ten PM dark, surrounded by candles,
extending her white petals,
the cereus is raising her head. The silence—complete.

One by one, we bend over the bloom, catching her fragrance.
She is lifting her skirts. And who would dismantle
the plant's white blossom.

In four hours, she will wilt, then die on her own,
and the garden will not be the same
for another year.

On the other side of the world,
the moon is flower.
Its white light beckoning.

To My Small Daughter
at one week

I lie in warm wheat fields,
welcome the first child,
pull her from my breast,
sniff her for afterbirth.

Over her forehead, I pass my tongue,
again over the tiny fists,
the perfect ten fingers.
I count her toes, twice,
brush my lips against the tufts
of hair that line the tops of her ears.
I clean the blood from her navel.
My kiss is healing to her eyes.

Her head sweeps back and forth
as a beast's does over grain,
finding my plain, my breast again.

> I shut my eyes here,
> begin to suck my tongue.

My Son Brings Bagpipe Music

Exuberance is beauty.
—William Blake

It fills the house. His house. My house.
   The church outside my back door.

Woods Park. The entire neighborhood.
   I never get enough & now it's been

too long. So I'm driving to find his music
   downtown, driving out O street, back on P,

     driving the way I do when he plays his bagpipe
        by the National Bank on 13th Street,

     the way I do when there's Blues in front of
        the Zoo Bar & the street's closed,

     the way I do when Jazz & Rock fill the intersection
        at 12th and N for July Jam,

I'm driving then circling back and around,
   trying to make all the stop lights because

a bank of white clouds is crowding out
   the moon in its blue heaven &

there's a storm coming & on this side of the street
   a vacant lot where cicadas & crickets are

harping on. Then suddenly on this summer night
   my son, echoing the God of Bagpipes

in the nimbus & thunderheads, completes all
   the extravagance and beauty I could ask for.

Sunday Afternoons
My Son Bakes Bread

makes it from scratch. Salt-free yeast bread,
whole wheat, plain white, and today,
Babka, my favorite. He prepares
two pans with a crumbled mix of butter,
sugar, and spices, then cuts the citron,
lemon and lime, for the dough

which has risen once, been punched down.
I make only fast breads. Irish soda bread, banana,
peanut butter, bourbon-pecan, Poor Poet's Bread.
All without yeast. Requiring no kneading.

Lost to the rest of us, his face down, smiling,
he becomes, though he'd frown at my saying it,
the boy I raised, focusing completely,
concentrating as he's done since a toddler; now

the six-foot four-and-a-half inch frame bent over
the floured board, working the dough, palms
shaping it, turning it around and around,
making two small loaves.

While they rise, we tell what's new;
as they bake, we swap stories.

Some call for a shot of rum over them
while cooling. He ignores this for now,
sends a loaf home with me. This treat.
This nurturing. Returning the favor.

To My Small Son
at three months

You awaken and
        quiet as the stars
you throw off light
        now light years away

as if the smile
        you will fix on a lover
          years hence
beckons
        from far and away
          beyond me

Last Night Dreaming and in the Dream Barbara Shows Me Her New Poem

In "Taking My Car to the Mechanic," she's going
to see the Doctor and on that day experiences
none of her long-standing complaints.

All in remission. The chronic rhinitis,
skin rash, headaches, irregular heart beats,
diarrhea, fatigue, arthritis, breast lumps.

Rattles, screeches, knocks all gone. A week later
they reappear with high pitched whining.
The repair shop can't work her in for another month.

I close that dream, get out of bed,
go to the fridge for a glass of orange juice,
listen to rain in the hackberry tree.

A person in middle life: an old car?
Transmission, choke and clutch going out?
slowly, but definitely, running low on oil,

finally burning out? Or an old tree leaning
away from the wind? A piece of ripe
and rotting fruit, a guava maybe?

She would say none of these. And I too:
We go back to Ether, go back to the Light.
       Tabula Rasa.

Next day, just as the sun sets for real,
I call Barbara. She's well. So am I.
I don't tell her about her sick car poem.

Magic Slim on the Radio
in memory, W. F.

"Nothin' But The Blues" on KSKA
in Anchorage, Alaska, with Magic Slim & The Tear Drops
and the whole Zoo Bar in Lincoln, Nebraska,
pews around the black walls,
a few chrome & plastic tables & chairs
& the long bar are all right here in my study

and the Zoo's room is dark, long & narrow
as a country church & I'm makin' some swings
on the Zoo's wooden floor with Warren Fine
who's forgettin' his new novel,
his student & his girlfriends for this
'cuz "HEY! The Blues is All Right!"

A Window
for JG

There is a legend that death
pulls the beat of the heart
back to earth again,
at home there

and there where you are looking
through the dark beyond the trees,
a light all night long.

No one but you
can part those branches.

The Siamese Cat Is Sleeping

This is my second poem about him.
The first one I don't let anybody read
because it's so damned clever.
In it, the cat is a chameleon with owl's ears,
a monkey's tail people-blue eyes,
and a seal's coat.

You know that kind of poem,
the kind of cat,
looking at you like a Sphinx,
remembering more about you
than meets the eye.

I this poem the cat is simply old,
"Old Man" I call him,
once bred to be the watchdog of Siam
now fat, no longer sleek.

He's round and ragged,
would look right in place in a painting
by Thomas Benton who probably
never painted cats; but never mind,
because at eight-four he said about death,
"I don't give a damn. I make no moves
in contemplation toward death."

And recently I heard it said
that Siamese cats
tend to go off in a corner
and sleep their way there.

Bird Song
for my mother, my father

By the time I look up
        they are gone
On the asphalt
        shadows of two pigeons
              lifting off

From Weeping Water

Ahead a feedlot steams;
two miles back the cement factory
shrouds Weeping Water in its dust
and where Pawnees finding it easy
to worship once paused on horses,
a mist rises from the snow.

On the horizon, Lincoln Electric
sends up signals no one reads.
Inside I imagine a Pawnee
leans on a boiler, smokes a cigarette.

He sees wind through tall grass,
Buffalo feeding on wildflowers
where even Prairie Dog, Owl,
and Rattlesnake have homes.

The Four-Quartered Universe

A thousand years from here
buffalo run in the bluestem.
Pawnees move their earth lodges
where Genoa, Nebraska, sleeps,
the morning star not yet risen.

Cut off from a long past on this land,
I shift back to my grandmother's
German Black Forest, see her throwing
white sheets on the meadow to bleach.

Something builds from the center,
my song reluctant and quiet.

By the *Kits-Ka-Toos* (the Platte)

In June the children came from Oklahoma
to stand for the first time in the sacred water.

Now it is twenty below. My breath turns to fire—
the river, burned by December, to bones of ice and smoke.

Wind from the Dakotas slips through the cottonwoods.
Overhead ride branches feathered with hoarfrost,

Pawnee hunters on horseback, their women gone
into the trees, the old ones flinging white hair

in the sun to dry. I look again: the *Kits-ka-toos*
is breathing. Beneath it the roots of the trees grow deep.

View of Pawnee Origins

Before Coronado walked the bend of the Arkansas
        upstream from Lindsborg
        or the Wichita left pueblos
        to settle in grass houses and tipis;

before their women were tattooed,
        or the boy and his dog
        turned to red stone near Nemaha;

before the animals came to their water homes,
        the *Nahu 'rac* near Guide Rock;

beneath a place called *Wiharu*, in the sky,
        place of "wonderful things,"
        where corn ripens and parfleches
        of buffalo meat were stored,

this wide prairie looked up to see the springs
        of all life and I look beyond
        what the stories give,
        above the head and heart,
        the aches of thought,
        all our black nights.

Over these crows that rest in the dusk
        and corn stubble, the first gleam
        came through a chink in the early silence

before night, the people, the Morning Star.

By the Nelchina

The early stars are coming
through the first darkening.

Against this same sky
    (lit as it is by a low, full moon),

the black spruce and yellow birch
    (turned to shadow)

call into question
any absolute answers.

The fire in the stars may have died
being years away. The grandmothers'

and grandfathers' name are in black
or in stone. Turn. Fall asleep.

In this valley, the sounds of the river
fall back on themselves and keep going.

Fragments Concerning the Canopic Jars

Take away the net curtains
               and behold: light
                             coming from the ashes.

*

Forgive us for disturbing
               your delicious loneliness,
                             the edge of a far away sadness.

*

Who will return,
               will read
                             the sacred annals?

*

All good luck is dust.
No one know now what to ask for.
                         Somewhere behind the moon
                             the star you wished on has crashed.

*

Now shining,
               the moon comes soon
                             after sunset erasing starlight.

*

The fall to age is swift.
               Ascension, then the descent.
                             Arc of a javelin.

*

What was overheard
               was not
                             what was understood.

Girl Talk (paper)

Told me I was nuts to give up beating out
my woes on the piano to take up with words
no one heard. Just slipping them in this place
out that envelope. And besides, she said,
you never sing or even hum anymore and you
don't talk to me much at lunch
but you sure are a good listener
and if I had to have a sister I'd choose you
losers are the talkers and takers and I'm talkin'
and takin' you to lunch today my treat
but if I thought I could play even chopsticks
I wouldn't be sittin' here I'd be home
practicin'.   And I'll tell you, reader,
as I didn't tell her, how it was for me
tracing the prints my grandmother left
on the keyboard, how it was both making
and hearing the rise and fall of cadences,
going over and over those wordless entreaties,
resolutions, the *tierce de Picardies*, nocturnes,
Nice. It was nice. No words. Purity.

And the listening continues here in the blue
light of dusk, in the sound of a pen
scratching on paper, of paper sliding
against paper like those illicit flirtations
where more goes on despite AIDS than the woman
and the man will admit, how reaching for his glass
he brushes the hair on my arms and the hair
stands up all over my body. His touch like the word
most loved: "home"—carrying it everywhere
and with an appetite for whatever occurs to me,

writing it true as though it were possible,
as though one could answer where the music goes,
where the embrace goes, when it is finally over.

1 AM poem

quiet here   writing letters   notes

  postcard poems   revising

    some of the best of friends

        on paper

Friends, These Gifts

A handful of snow, throw it into the air.
And the first stars cutting the sky,
These, too, another celebration.

Now look at your hands. Are they your mother's?
Your father's? And who else has marked your life?
When I consider my collection of heart-shaped stones—
Some small and red, other black and broken, a few
The size of my fist—I know those hearts I've shared.

For you, come Spring, I'll put the feather
Of some bird who flew through the nearby trees
Or a leaf onto the plate with the stones.
Or into an envelope and mail it.

3 Love / Work / Travel

To let the self be awakened
by all things is enlightenment

Dōgen (1200–1253)

Girl Talk (aristotle)

Told me so much I finally broke my silence,
told her when in the middle of life
you're an orphan, both parents dead,
with no lover, friends dying of love
and AIDS, when looking down and away
from some plateau to better see the seashore
or the shadow of yourself deep in some box canyon,
then what? The obvious so real it rarely gets said,
as Aristotle wrote? Aristotle who, after all,
abhorred the way music manipulates emotion,
and us remembering Mozart, putting in a CD—
his Fantasia in C Minor.

                       Told her forget
everything but making art, get to your studio,
new images. And focus, give yourself to paint again,
forget the men, your delicious melancholy
is eating you up, you need to feed it,
with color maybe.

                       She answered: charcoal
and I'd like to go back to the door with that one
good man behind it. Then she shook her head.

I told her the older we get, the more complex.
Life, too? We can't redo the past?
We had the experience but somehow we missed
the meaning?

                       Told me the two AM soul
goes solo sorry babe gotta run
my head's full of feathers at this hour.

And as abruptly as a darting sparrow, she left.
No parting shot, no words, only whistling.

Girl Talk (light)

Libraries, she growled, make me very nervous
the way some teenage girls at the mall do
so many voices screaming to be heard

art galleries fuel my dreams
your poetry books bring them too
but I don't go to book warehouses.

It seemed she was about to pick up on the old
argument between us: images in words vs.
visual images in paint—until her last line,

More light, she said, Goethe's words
on his deathbed you and I the light
in our lines on canvas on paper
in our work in our friendships *more light!*

(How did *she* know that quote?
      Well, light enough!
            I let it go.)

Girl Talk (room / for writing)

The poem is never finished,
it is merely abandoned
        —Paul Valéry

Pointing out the volunteer asparagus fern,
    growing outside the closed window
in the deep window well, I say welcome.

    Hummph, she hummed upon entering, just
a clutter of paper and books to me, she said,
    like any executive's messy business office.

    (We agree to disagree and we are friends.)
I protested, look on the shelves, the walls:
    masks—of black feathers, of red satin,

of blue beads and sequins, a silver half-moon mask,
    And others. The *Mask*, I emphasized.
(She didn't get it.) Protesting too much, I continued

    my list of elegant things: the black fan
from Spain, the wreath from a croning,
    the poetry and art postcards, the poetry calendars,

the blue ceramic sugar bowl filled with lavender,
    the books and their spines—*objets d'art*:
umbre, beige, cerulean blue, wine-colored,

    mauve, cochineal red, magenta, Irish green,
royal purple, orange, white, black. And
    the fine art handset letterpress books,

some with covers of linen from Holland,
    poetry texts on French handmade papers,
handsewn signatures, limited editions and, I said

    with my voice falling, also destructible,
fugitive paperbacks and hardbacks,
    (at "fugitive," she smiled),

three desk tops covered with notes, letters,
   abandoned drafts, reworked
final drafts, manuscripts in separate piles,

   a few papers underfoot,
(I whispered the Paul Valéry quote),
   the work I should burn or shred,

and announcements for books and readings
   propped on bookshelves against volumes
of poetry and art, music and history,

   fiction, philosophy, and more.
(If I *need* it, I find it. If I *want* it, I find it)
   But everyone, she said, has papers and books

not everyone has paints palettes canvases
   boxes of beads feathers dried flower petals
frames not everyone has brushes the smell

   of paint and turpentine here's the stale odor
of papers and books the bookworms eating away
   but I appreciate your work, the poems

heart made visible spirit incarnate
   here's only another book warehouse
gimme your finished poems my friend

   now I'm outta here, she insisted
while I was pulling up something
   intangible to her, pulling it

up by the roots, the form growing
   its own way, like a plant.
She turned, and must have seen something, because

   (with a nod at the photos on the desk
of AIDS victim Fred, friends
   and family from far away, long ago,

one of me and a former husband,
   baby pictures of my son and daughter,
two granddaughters, two Siamese cats)

>   she took from her bag
> a pencil and sketch pad,
>   and she began to draw.

Girl Talk (trash)

She holed herself up in her studio for a while,
painting. After a couple of weeks
of not wanting my company she called.

Told me: I miss my long-standin' lover
(and I don't mean my good buddy Fred)
said he wanted to think us through
took off travelin' haven't heard from him
now a month of Sundays or more
and it isn't only the scent of his chest
and hair his sexual warmth I miss
in the morning it's no hello glad you're
alive my world's wonderful with you in it
that deep voice and him to make coffee for
put on some Mozart for all that daily trash
I miss, she said, that makes my art
so one-dimensional so sterile.

Girl Talk (tracings)

Told me: these lines as you see them

will go down the left margin

of that water color

titled "California Tide"

    "Touch me"

        I said
        while his hand
        was moving
        across my thigh
        like a wave
        and he said

    "I am touching you"

        but something
        (the moon?)
        had washed the touch
        from his eyes
        they moved
        across the room
        as though it were
        a shoreline
        and he seemed
        to be making
        tracings
        over me
        as if I
        were sand

Card Player

Keeps the chin down.
No one sees the downcast eyes
are proud between the deals.
Keeps the cards of his dreams
close to his chest.
No chance of their being shuffled
or redealt.
The first round stands pat.
He's out before he's in.
Whispers cover his path,
slap his hands.

The table folds,
the house collapses.
But he slouches his frame
around the fist-clenched heart,
waits in agony at the thought
of Lady Luck straddling him.
How to raise the chin after all
this practice?
How to let the arms fall free
at the side, then lift
to scoop up the kitty?

Girl Talk (Standing-in-Blue-Flags Painting)

shallow marshland, wet meadow
    under bits of blue sky, cumulus clouds
under an orchard of blossoming apple trees
    half sun, half shade

slowly passing through this country
    husband and wife, and still lovers
        driving near Haines, Oregon,
            to friend Dorik's place

a small herd of Holstein cows
    grazing in blue flags
their udders touching the flowers

    *

Told me:

twenty years ago burned into memory
none of these any longer together

though each another gone thing
    I can't I won't lose 'em

Girl Talk (Another-Little-Love-Poem Painting)

Told me, pointing, this text going around
all sides of that black and white abstract
a mix of Pollock Franz Kline Barbara Kreuger
the calligraphy's like Persian script
with a scattering of dried wild rose petals:

>*over and over*
>*the unfaithful lovers says:*
>
>*if you came back*
>>*I would kiss*
>
>*your eyelids*
>>*you beautiful animal*
>
>*the water is deep*
>>*and next time*
>
>*I would see*
>>*into its depths*

Told her: A beautiful object:
>*the flowers of possibility.*

Girl Talk (poetry / reading)

After my recent reading told me she wanted
her hand on the back of his head the man
sitting in front of her in the coffee house
with his long-haired girlfriend who wouldn't give him
as much as one glance, she said, he was
beginnin' to massage her upper arm
the small of her back and above her scoop-neck
white crocheted sweater below the paisley scarf
tied loosely around her throat he began strokin'
her bare skin slowly dippin' his head
into that soft place between her head and
shoulder restin' it there a moment
long enough for me to sketch him

his warm breath probably fragrant
with espresso and, she continued, I began
caressin' my own left knee didn't know
what else to do with my left hand 'n his cheek
against her cheek 'n I wanted to blow in his ear
but I settle for tryin' a mock nude-descendin'-
the-staircase-style sketch and, she said,
I started suckin' my own tongue.

Told her as Anne Sexton said, though
in another context, "about nineteen in the head."
She missed the joke, my accent on first syllable
of Sexton, or didn't hear it and she blathered on:

I tried concentratin' again on my sketch
but your poetry your words were comin' through
I did my kegel exercises to the cadences
my mind in a *ménage a trois* he was nibblin'
her ear. See, here's the sketch, what'cha' think.

Yes, I said, I see myriad influences and
asked how much of my reading she caught.

She began another sketch, forgot my poetry
for the moment, capturing her feelings
      on the white, silent paper.

Girl Talk (heart / meditation)

Told her take a deep breath
        while counting six heartbeats.

Hold
        for eight heartbeats.

Then let it go, let it all out
        for six or eight heartbeats.

Repeat sequence fifteen minutes.
        *

Then
        you return
                to the home
                      of your spirit.

Or not.
        All same.

Girl Talk (bosh / save)

Asked me if roses are roses are roses
isn't it so much flapdoodle and bosh
that you write and I sketch and paint
if things are as they are? We were sitting,
in the picnic shelterhouse at a local park
trying to figure out how we came this far.

Told her sometimes to capture, reclaim
whatever seems almost lost, nearly gone—

like *cupolas*, domes on top of old barns,
worth a line or two, a thousand images.
At times it seems as if one is atop
my head funneling in light, shining.

She contemplated the circular bandstand
across the street in the town square,
soon to fall down—the missing steps
and railings, the chipped paint—although
she wasn't sketching. And I wasn't writing.

I could save the bandstand later. Some days
life was too fast for pencil and paper.
Or too slow. She left and I sat for a while
waiting for my soul to catch up before going
to my study, before using pencil over paper
where white is obliterated in places,
black with illumination—
       table, chair, bed, home.

Girl Talk (leaving)

That winter, after I recited my "Maalox Moment"
about locking myself out of the house
wearing only my Eddie Bauer down robe
and slippers, just checking the 11:30 PM
snow still coming down at eight below,
how I went next door to the widow Myra
knowing she'd be awake watching TV,
how I used her phone to call the landlord
who brought his key, not disturbed at all
to help a damsel in the cold, she told me,

don't know what a "Maalox Moment" is
guess I don't have 'em don't watch TV
hate rock'n roll country western too
but wanna learn country swing dancin'
find a trucker travel across the west
nevada utah new mexico get to know
the desert draw *saguaros* so manly
and nights so cold can't get on the wavelength
of yuppies dicks whoever they are.
I'll cash in my T Bonds buy a stand-up-
in-van learn harmonica maybe guitar take
voice lessons, she said, since my lover left
an' buddy Fred died feel like I gotta
get away gotta get away, she sang.

When I stopped by her studio, she was sketching
a cactus, letting her hair grow long and lank
and straight. No more curls, she told me,
had a lover said I might as well put a bone
through my nose as have my hair
rolled up in a home perm and he
was right he said I might as well stop
tryin' to be a fem fer men and
get on truckin' down route 66.

She lit a cigarette, looked into the smoke
and told me, even smoke leaves a shadow.

Why

are you
      casting your line
           into fast moving waters

when there
      in the small quiet pool
           the one in shadow

you are
      the one fish
           you must catch

Girl Talk (nine / 9)

Last time I saw her a few years back
before she went west to work the *saguaros*,
told me what goes around, goes around and around
and around and never seems to come around.
And she stopped talking about her love life,
the sad and occasional rolling down of a condom,
how perhaps her body had outlived its curiosity,
its instinct for pushing forward her sexual energy.
She stopped smoking, stopped stopping in
for girl talk and happily began taking prizes
for her drawings. And here I am, seeing
nine the unfinished number, wondering when or if
she'll drop me a card with her current address.

And me, tied to my barn, teaching, writing,
smoking, forgetting about rescues myself,
me skirting the rough edges of AIDS, thinking love
may be the last of the serious childhood diseases.

Though the night is warm and sensual,
the crescent moon showing her seductive smile
of promise, my bed remains empty. Fuck it, I say.
as she has. But finally, no: pencil and paper,
I say, for both of us; love, that temporary stay
against solitude; and art, too, the long reaches,
those arduous, amorous rides drawing us
toward and into whatever objects and subjects
the spirit/mind/heart, the body craves.

Christmas Letter from Alaska

Dear Friends,
Night comes early here
and the stars I see
may not be visible to you.
I remember New Year's Eve in Uxmal
I searched the sky for Ursa Major
but the Bear was north
over Washington, Wyoming and Nebraska,
within your sight then as now.
Imagining Bethlehem's star
I became seven again at the Christmas pageant,
the Madonna swathed in blue,
invisible promise in her arms.
I wanted to be her, the serene one,
pondering in my heart the secrets I could keep.
These days I want to share them:
the light falls to its knees on the floor;
night at the window moves toward me;
on the horizon one star will slip away
with another tilt of the earth.
Friends, the world spins
in a wind we do not understand;
there are constellations not found
by any eye. Yet there is the Word.
Set loose within our view,
these words would bring it.
I send you this love,

December Notes

The backyard is one white sheet
Where we read in the bird tracks

The songs we hear. Delicate
Sparrow, heavier cardinal,

Filigree threads of chickadee.
And wing patterns where one flew

Low, then up and away, gone
To the woods but calling out

Clearly its bright epigrams.
More snow promised for tonight.

The postal van is stalled
In the road again, the mail

Will be late and any good news
Will reach us by hand.

Juan de Fuca, Port Townsend

A sailboat from Point Hudson
heads into the Straits, a honey bee
for wildflowers at the water's edge.

Grey driftwood had found its place,
this string of morning light.

Wright's Beach, Northern California

Two AM

Awake from a dream,
the words so strange
I don't recall them.

The gibbous moon perhaps.
The sound of the ocean
on the rim of the world.

I light a small fire for coffee,
but can't shut out the tide,
won't shut out the moon.

The friends I have
would understand.

Six AM

I wait for the rock I call
The Temple of the Magician
emerging from the mist.

At dusk the Temple was golden.
"None but the peregrine
shall climb me," it proclaimed.

My steps in wet sand,
the tide has taken
all but seven.

Now a sea otter
travels parallel to me,
asks what I am doing
so far from home.

At the water's edge, I take
another seven steps toward him,
my footprints go with
the next wave.

Hands

The hands at the end of your wrists are not your hands.
They swing far from the heart with its cold streams,
from the head with its warm rushes, and
when you walk you are going away from the hands,
they can never keep up,
they want to get away, to get back to old clasps
or to go forward beating through the wide rivers.
They are never satisfied to stay with you and
go swinging like gates in the wind.
Though your arms hold them hinged
at some point you are walking fast away from them
in the direction of hands.

4 Space

Things That Are Near Though Distant

Sei Shonagon, c. 990

Girl Talk (negative / space)

Told me (though it took over a year and came
in a letter):

dear sister of my heart, been thinkin' about
your good talk on the one good man
and ever since mine left i'm thinkin' negative space
and the way one line leads to another
then finally there's an end or there's

a subtle movement the way the shadow
of a dry bouquet in moonlight coming through
a window shifts in time on a wall

or the line might lead to a <u>caution:</u>

> the briar rose (see enclosed sketch of same
> dropping some of its petals) how all at last
> falls away yet somehow stays permanent
> as change becoming <u>memory</u> becoming
> simply another <u>text</u> before becoming <u>dust</u>

let me know how you respond to the sketches
the images especially the <u>saguaro</u> anthropomorphic
and phallic growing solidly from earth yet bound
just as a sturdy woman is to <u>what</u> is

and what about adding some text scrawled
in calligraphy on my french rives papers:

> - 'oh, what's the word I'm searchin' for?' —
> - 'love' = 'rose' = 'embrace' = 'muse' =
> - 'bell' = 'smooth fur' = 'more than a word' =
> - 'each' : 'tongue on skin': 'hand on thigh':
> - 'a pair of lips': 'a glance': 'each':
> - 'a spell in one beat' = 'a note'
> - 'these gifts': 2 = 1: & + = ++

i'll scatter 'em saunchwisekaddywampus
just a line or two across each in this series
it's titled 'comin' back home again'

and i <u>am</u> comin' back in <u>just a few months!!</u>

These ideas for the larger work
should be ready for the opening in four weeks
what'cha think? ya comin' out or <u>what?</u>

> P.S.   i want to work in some dried petals
>
> P.P.S. the road to hell paved with lilacs
> wild roses wild plum blossoms
> he said he'd bring to me and <u>didn't</u>
>
> i was only so much impasto to him—
> he's just another layer of pentimento to me—
>
> someone said they heard he has hiv
>
> i'm devastated—<u>i'm working</u>—i'm returning

She neither signed the letter nor wrote
her name above the Arizona address, but
there's no mistaking who it's from—not
with that lingo, those run-ons, underlinings,
the affectation of no letters in caps,
her swirling calligraphy, her exuberance
and, in the art piece text, the oblique messages.

Girl Talk (lists)

Now that she's back, I visited her in her studio
and she asked me what'cha readin'? I showed her
the list of "Elegant Things" in Sei Shonagon's
Pillow Book come down to us from tenth-century Japan,
and she said,

                I work from my own list
those things that look beautiful in sunlight

snow fallin' and tiny blue flowers on the rosemary
in my east kitchen window and shadows
of clouds floatin' on the river over fields
green winter wheat a rain storm
the single tear in my buddy Fred's left eye
just before he died of AIDS and
through a sunny window a meadow
of snow that no animal nobody not even me
had ever stepped into and

any of my sunlit paintings will fit in
with my impressionistic washes my visions
so what's on your list, she asked.

Told her maybe I'd write from her list!
And I add sounds and smells. Mourning doves
calling at dawn, the fragrance of mock orange
in bloom, ambulance sirens, soft wind
over wheat fields, spicy smells off the river,

and my mother coming out of the bathroom
laughing and saying it doesn't smell like roses
in there. And the jingle of my telephone, voices
of my adult son or daughter, my two
granddaughters or friends on the other end,
sun and moon eclipses, my two brothers.

She picked up her brushes. I walked
into the bright afternoon, humming.

Girl Talk (music / purity)

Told me I could develop my writing by playing
the piano again. Told me: *Music, the purest
of all art forms.*
                      I was thinking not purity
but heart speaking to heart as in Beethoven,
as in the Blues, as in Thelonius Monk.

You had a good start, she blurted out,

then you moved down a rung or two
to slippery words gave up the piano.

I asked, Perhaps mantras—wouldn't that be
more pure? And what about love poems.
Told her the love poem may be talking
to itself alone. Maybe all poetry
does that, for the music of it.

She spouted how about playin' this upright
just a little bit of Mozart Bach?
Try playin' the piano again 'n then
just lay the music out there in poems
don't try to mean somethin' just present it
the way music 'n my sketches do
that's purity the reader finds the meanin'.

Told her you really tick me off when you harp
on music and lecture me on aesthetics
I already know. Besides we don't
see things as they are anyway;

we see thing the way *we* are. So do you
want Dame Edith Sitwell's "Facade?"

It was no use debating, trying to convince her
I wouldn't play her piano—a waste
of words, so I began studying another
of her AIDS quilt panels. She was stenciling
children's names on it, the many names.

Girl Talk (lazy / domestic)

Told me in the record book she's had
since the seventh grade, the quote *Not lazy
just domestic* marked her birthdate.

Seems true, she said, me frittering away
the time in my studio even at home
seeing only what's right in front of me
the shape and color of the marble top tables
each speck of dust on the mirror the desk
the shape and colors of dried roses crystal
and everyday glassware in the sunny kitchen and

never mind he died years ago
my father's hands, she said, like those
in the painting praying hands and
when he looked at me he saw me

Be the thing you see his favorite quote

    Rest easy Friend. Rest in the Light,
the text on Fred's memorial quilt panel.

What We're Doing, First and Foremost,

writes Colette, *when we seek friendship*
    or give it is to cry: 'Sanctuary! Sanctuary!'
        That cry . . . the best thing in us.

The gift of presence, fragrant as cinnamon,
    dry leaves of sycamore, ritual applause,
        a cloister for celebration.

Of sanctuary, Colette advised
    that we keep the rest dark
        as long as we possibly can.

       *

Shape of a friend, guise of a foreigner.

    The one, and the other.

Girl Talk (high / bird)

Told me had a friend so high-strung
if she'd let go his at a concert
he'd rise to the rafters, a helium balloon.

A dancer, she said, he seemed to lift off
en pointe tap skylarking or waltzing
one of those boys light on his feet

everything in the highest register
no one could match his obligato his steps
'n laugh that fella could laugh at anything
the announcement I'd been practicin' yoga
on 'n off for twenty years had him snortin'
as if it were a mantra however he couldn't sit
couldn't meditate but he could concentrate

never saw a fella so reluctant to give up
on a good joke even when it was on him
even when not really a joke but a slur
like someone callin' out hey you faggot
he'd treat it as if it were a jest

even when in the last stages of the plague
he never lost his *joie de vivre*

went out of state to die like an old
sparrow crawled off to hide in the shade
of some low spirea or currant branches
his wings his feet finally stilled although
something remained suspended floating

and I've asked homophobics, she told me,
what if he'd been a son or a brother
how could anyone be against anyone

so giving so high-spirited so full of malarkey
blue mud the old blarney.

Girl Talk (after images)

Told me, gesturing: it's from a dream.

The lines, written in calligraphy, turquoise ink,
over a perpendicular, blue-green abstract
I take to be my friend's self-portrait,
much like Max Ernst's portrait of his wife,
Dorothea as I recall, his with no text.

*

    field   hill
     (til/till)   (climb)
      plant/
      harvest

*

    thicket   plain
    (berries)   (graze)

*

    river   tree
    (fish/   (climb/
    drink   hide)

*

    meadow   stone
    (flowers)   (think)

*

    fence   gate
  (stay/climb) (go shut)

*

    bird   cat

      (choose)

Girl Talk (Dream-and-Love-Collage-with-Text)

Told me my collage goes with your poem
and we'll hang 'em side by side OK?

"The Coral Reefs We Rest On,
Caves of Abandoned Hyrozoans":

> *A connoisseur of good tunes*
> *dreams sea anemones,*
> *takes me to Majorca.*
> *Fifteen years richer*
> *and older than I*
> *wants me to marry,*
> *lets me take lovers.*
> *Knowing none surpass him*
> *I give them back to foam.*
> *Now I lie abed nude*
> *in a place of ferns*
> *as warm as Key West.*
> *He, next to me a poet.*
> *Poor as I, though younger.*
> *We live on the sands we write daily,*
> *go to the dock,*
> *fish as rarely as possible.*
> *I, with the ovaries of a lobster,*
> *think and choose. My future*
> *floats: plants rooting in water*
> *or pens feathering to fly.*
>
> *How can I choose? You*
> *fathering sea lavender?*
> *Dying in a fading rose color? Me*
> *resting my head against limbs?*
> *A young Key lime?*
> *An olive tree?*

Girl Talk (dream lines / frescoes)

Who knows what frescoes   *Do not forget that a poem*
are inside the human skull   *even if it is composed*
   —William Blake   *in the language of giving information,*
                                   is not used in the language game
                                   of giving information
                                          —Wittgenstein

To stare into the water and not see a face

The memory   when I came back   didn't improve

Mirror images of my husbands didn't come true

We held the light   green branches   bending down around us

People are only   as wise   as they are pollinated

Go away   til all the tangles   are gone

The space   that your absence   makes in me   so empty

                     She says
he spoke   like a dream
                     running

In the leaves   I meet myself   Let the light be brilliant

Lines before Sleep

Over this bridge
my voice long silent
I pause
drop words into water
like stones

A single note of bird song
drops from a bush
one red berry

Flowers and Friends
for all of them, 1992

They accompany me for a walk in the Sunken Garden
        Loving the early morning cool, the bright sun,
The slow jaunt. Nancy, Robin, and Keighley,
        In truth awakening in Las Cruces, pause with me
At the pond, its white and gold carp coming up
        A few at a time to gulp air and small water bugs.
And we are bending now over Impatiens growing tall
        After last night's good, hard rain, loving the shade,
The burst of white, red and fuchsia, stopping now
        At the small waterfall, its hullabaloo above
                The rise and fall of rush hour traffic.

Jim, though he walks the hills, the woods, the gardens
        Half a continent away, inveigles me to sit
In contemplation of the majestic, weed-like Zinnias,
        Drink our take-out cappuccinos, just a short break
Before breaking across the four-lane for Roses
        In the Triangle Garden where seven bronze blocks
Rise two stories high, cascading with water,
        Drowning the woosh of car wheels at seven A.M.

Hugging her pillow or a lover three hours behind us
        In Anchorage, Karen gives out with her bawdy laugh
At the bare-chested male jogger whose shorts are brief,
        His legs briefer, "Another square Adonis? Where's
A California hunk?" Sara, in Anchorage, too, enjoins,
        "Hey, it's a man! Come back here, Honey!"

Nancy and Robin cast a forlorn look our direction
        And, impatient to study the Roses, stick their noses
                Down and observe, "Some don't even have fragrance."

I look around, Jim's gone. And they all are going
        Away, one by one, the ones I haven't named here, too—
Friends in Crete, Minneapolis, London, Omaha,
        Etc., etc. And I've finished relating the news

To them, the news I've said so often in my head
        But never get around to writing. And, no, we won't
Have lunch, won't hear the Blues at the Zoo Bar,
        Nor witness thunderclouds coming exquisitely across
The plains. They've given up on me, on ever
        Hearing my voice, seeing me, receiving a letter of mine.

Names like Joanne and Dan, Geranium, their long friendship.
        Karen, Paula, Greg and Barb, Honeysuckle, generosity.
Cindy and Abby, John and Bernie, Katherine and Catherine,
        Not to forget David, Carol and Moriah,
Fair winds above these blooms. Names like Owen and Mary,
        Max and Hal, Max and John, Alice and Jack, Barbara and
Jim, Barbara and Bob, Cabbage Roses, those ambassadors of
        Love. Names like Jack and Jack, Coneflower and Coneflower,
Sunny herbs of the prairie. Francesco, James, Ted, Bachelor Buttons.
        Ingeborg, shadowy, cool Dusty Miller and Sage.
Betty, Gloria and Tom, true-blue Delphinium, and
        Chamomile, Bee Balm, Feverfew, their healing powers.
David, Robin, Candice, Caitlin, faithful Blue Violets.
        And how pleasant the company of old friends.

I give them these flowers, these fragrances,
        The past of fallen waters, names like Blue Flags,
And walk out of the garden as instinctively and
        Empty-headed as two cats I know, cats named
Rose and Tulip, truly they are, who would be
        Dazzled by the Cecropia Moths, big as Hummingbirds,
But that's another story. You know—friends
        like Meadow Lark, Blue Gill. Friends like Oceans,
Bordering the continents of our neighboring solitudes.
        Friends. Like Sand Hills. Friends. Like Mountains.

In David City Park
for Barbara

Under rain on the tin roof,
in the shelter house beside the lake,
sparrows coast and rest on beams
above two writers—women, each
with notebook open, pencils aside
and waiting, word by word
discussing the extravagance of rain,

the steady fall of its music overhead,
and, though we are primarily poets,
some words set down by fiction writers
Gina Berriault and Grace Paley,

how their words make poetry and music.
Then, we turn to how some folks,
despite AIDS, take pleasure in making
love randomly—we are reminded of this
daily, our primary concern: our children.

Our conversing, like the birds: now here,
now there, trusting on impulse,
improvisation. Our speaking nature
everywhere like the rain, the right
configuration of weather patterns
and proximity. A rhythm we come
to accept. Like any season.
The writing, coming later.

Girl Talk (sky / sleep)

Mixing paints on a saucer when I arrived,
she instructed me:

> *Orrrrange crrrries forrrrr blue*

had an art teacher from holland said that
so when I go to the park and I lie
on my back before I peel 'n eat my orange
I hold it up against the autumn blue sky

sometimes at sunset, she said, small puffs
of clouds and large drifting ones invade
the blue canvas images echoing those colors

pink orange peonies and great phoenixes
glowing flames ships afire
a film maker could document 'em
but I fall asleep then later carry
the colors and shapes home by heart
orrrange crrries forrr blue, she repeated,

the sky made of nothin' but vapor 'n wind
like your words, which go everywhere.

> She continued mixing her pigments.
> I fell silent and back into my quiet,
> still life again, her last phrase echoing:

like music like dreams like rivers the sky.

Girl Talk (*reflets dans l'eau* / *debussy* / reflections)

Told me it was her version of shimmering on water.

And I told her my impression in the music
Of her painting, clear to me as her eyes:

The calm of blue heights over indigo depths.
And in between, cold water resting.

"Are they frozen," the woman asks, "the reflections?
Could we walk on tree tops across the lake?"

The man mumbles Rilke's words about two solitudes
That he'll stay where he is, he releases her hand.

Now, the wind rising, the man stepping back
From the shore. And the water, stricken,

The trees, the woman tossing in the reflection.
When she glances at him, he looks up beyond the trees.

The wind subsides. The woman peers down,
Her face falling. And there, beside her,

The man's likeness, also sinking.
Into the foam. The water. The sky.

The lowest notes. The high.

5 Lingo

> *. . . but poets should*
> *Exert a double vision . . .*
> *To see . . . distant things as intimately deep*
> *As if they touched them . . .*

from "Aurora Lee," Elizabeth Barrett Browning, 1857

> *"Yucatan" means*
> *"listen to what you say."*

Ernesto Diaz, 1975

Girl Talk (piano)

Told her when I was away for a gig in a new town,
the first night I awoke about three AM because
I'd been sobbing, coming up out of deep sleep
where I'd been out walking past an old house
where men were taking sledge hammers to an old upright,
where I'd been crying and hollering at them,
You can't *do* that to pianos! *Pianos* are like
animals! Pianos *are* animals! But the battering
didn't cease.

Asked her, what the gods abhor
they first drive out of their senses,
as Euripides noted?

Still, I continued, it pleases me to think
that a sly savagery enriches the nuances of art.

>   (And sometimes we ask ourselves
>   how well do we dream what we think?
>   Or do what we dream?)

Girl Talk (brain / dump)

Told me these hot humid days she stays
in her studio. Like you in your study,

she said, where we see a world so large
the galaxies condensed on canvas on the page

we see so much the microcosms magnified
that we never see them the same ever again

except in our minds, or framed or between
book covers all else not quite true but

often the world would say it walks away
from us when we walk away gladly each day

into our early morning fog and paper work
on the hottest of hazy summer days.

The Mailman

Dreaming over the years of women throwing
open their yellow filmy robes, ripping
curlers out of their hair, jumping out of
blue jeans, unflouring their aprons, and
undressing their mailboxes for him
he finds on Monday only the corner of an
envelope thrust halfway under a door.
The invitation reads: Hurry I have
only enough time left to pencil this note
the wind breaks at the glass.

The woman he sees through the curtains
lies crumpled like a wad of old poems,
her jaw limp and dry, eyes ajar like doors,
the bed of her hips and breast, still.
She has lain there since Saturday.

Girl Talk (crab)

"after I wade the shallow pond
my friends help me with my troubles"

Showed me, from one of her dream times,
the title and text of another blue-green print:

> look I've come all this way pushing
> waist-high water with my heavy thighs
> looking across the surface for their faces
>
> after they hold me I head back
> where the shadow of a man is turning
> into a crab, the menacing claws
>
> I think I can't go through all this
> to go back through what I know
> to what I knew and what I've been through
>
> what I must do looking down
> with each step on the uneven bottom
> now of this pond   but I go

Told her my brother knows someone who charges
his friends five dollars to listen to a dream.

Girl Talk (night bird)

Showed me the text in calligraphy from one
of her nightly dreams to accompany the best
of her monoprints from an all-night session
at the Visual Arts Center Press:

> *behind my eyes crossing the border*
>   *between waking and sleeping, the young*
> *sharp-shinned hawk runs down diagonally*
>   *from shadows on the far right horizon*
> *into the glaring light of the left foreground*
>   *wings flapping frantically above her head*
> *drumsticks pumping straight into my skull*
>   *where she works all night at flight*

Told me by morning she will never have left the ground.

Girl Talk (frames)

Lifted up the painting of a dream
with some words for her lover
scribbled in the margins around the work:

>   wanting to come back to your spaces
>   from where I slammed you shut last hour

>   I feel them out
>   my hand over the clear pane

>   you do not look up or notice
>   as the cat tries to pull off
>   the green-framed storm window

>   lashing at the glass
>   paws pulling at the sill

>   cramming the head into a crack of space
>   that would seem to be a beginning

Sleep Talk

I'm on the edge of sleep and
the bed tips out of balance.
With no sound of your turning,
your breath not here,
the room is unguarded.
Just now my dreams are of flying
and falling from helicopters,
then skimming in a jet twenty feet
above the ground in Minneapolis,
speeding between pillars
or monuments to famous men.
And I hear shattering
the expensive Swedish crystal
of a friend.

Girl Talk (dream / call)

Told me: he came here last night
the comforting beard bear-like form
in dream pieces of such puzzling
recollections I haven't seen him
for at least five hundred miles
these dozen years' distance haven't
talked to him since an August wind
blew through my hair with me
at the end of a telephone cord
in a booth with no door 95 degrees
on the highway outside Cheyenne
me thinkin' art him talkin' poems
posters readin' rodeo rodeo *roe-day-oe*

I finally drove east and away but
tonight just can't shake thinkin'
about where it all ends up no blue
ribbons no shoutin' no more rides

but a real cowgirl would toss it off
her hat in the air sayin' cheers and
next she'd open a brown bottle
            of Bud.

Love Poem

There is a soft place
between your neck and shoulder.
I move my face back and forth
in that dip
and shut my eyes.
I think it must be Ireland
or Scotland.
I've never been there,
but my eyes go up and down
those green glens
and every dip and incline
moves as we find our own ground.

Girl Talk (passion / mind)

Got so she repeated herself so often,
the next time she mouthed that one-good-man
monologue and said she was dead as a woman
without him, I told her no use trying to
find him, you've both changed, never
the same river twice because time overtakes us
the way the shadow of a hill or a slow wind
comes one tree at a time and embraces us.

So take courage, Friend, I said, and patience.
The shadow of the roof finally engulfed
the window in the early morning hours
when the full moon drifted west and away.
What can I say but that we slip imperceptibly
from passion to the mind though somehow aware
of it in our genitals and breasts. Told her the eye
teaches the mind or is it the other way around
when one man or even the memory of many
integrates the desires of body and brain.

She listened and said, when you talk those
comparisons, I see only Fred dying
of AIDS and some dead-black strobe lights
so babe let's hit the bars and look
for the good long look and the slow dance
I'm so lonely for in the body.

Telling her to go to her studio and paint
would have been manipulation and wasting
my imagination. She'd have said, Fuck it.
And she did anyway.

Fuck it I'm outta here, she told me.

Girl Talk (super h'way)

Asked me, Art 'n Poetry on the internet?
She shook her head and a finger at me.

Told her *What most people call reality,
the maximum of irreality,* Max Eastman.
Again pursuing my trivia: Robert Browning:
Works done least rapidly, Art most cherishes.

And, she pontificated, what the eye beholdeth
the hand hath made it also holdeth our works
on paper   one of a kind   save for books

Her final words on the subject, arms
crossed, nose pushed high in the air.
She sniffed and she left.

Girl Talk (difficult)

After being difficult, she told me:

I really don't know what to say
just feelin' my way to it
a word at a time 'n maybe
the right one'll plunge out
awkward as a fledgling bird
from its nest

starting over   another try

flying with a blind spot
is not that easy

*

That was as close as she came
to saying sorry. And I've forgotten
what it was she said or did.

Friends.

Girl Talk (letter / love)

Told me she gave up counting lovers,
puts a tape under her pillow most nights,
an old lover talkin' a love letter at me,
she said, from fifteen years ago
a hot pad on my back in winter
in summer a pillow I make as if cars
going by are the sounds of the surf
on Big Sur and the fan is only a fan,
she said, for God's sake let's keep cool.

Sleeps with the shades up so when the moon
comes by she'll see it. Told me she's got
no poetry in her soul but maybe night's
the time for it, said she's hungry for it,

maybe because she's on a diet or maybe
because she heard a fat man at a salad bar
mumble, fat man ain't 'pose to eat, and
under his breath, fat man ain't 'pose to fuck.

Forget AIDS, she told me, there's got to be
more than that when it comes to eatin'
when it comes to havin' a lover—agreed?
don't'cha think? she asked, don't'cha'gree?

Girl Talk (monarchs)

Told me she'd go bonkers if she had to stay
in that house all alone a whole weekend.

At 5 PM every Friday had to get in the car
to watch the country roll by. Some things
had to move in this world and by god, she'd
be one of them. The town was dead and so many
of her lovers and friends, didn't want to stick around
because of all the memories, and all the memories
would be lost in time anyhow, so let's go, she said.

She went alone to shopping malls,
flea markets, movies, fast food joints,
just to stay ahead of what plagued her.

Practicing reality, she told me, fantasy
was back there in the routines of teaching,
cleaning, shopping, dancing.

I was listening and thinking that,
in those years, fantasy was her sister.

She continued: ya shoulda' seen those two deer
leap up and away in front of the Chevy van
ahead of me on the way to the city. Told me
monarchs all matin' and driftin' and hawks
coilin' down waitin' to dive, all of them
too dangerous too erotic to sketch right now.

Girl Talk (eternity)

Told me she and her best friend went shopping
last Saturday and her pal bought the expensive perfume
Eternity.

                Is that a charm? I asked,
Does any love last an eternity? Jaded
about long-lasting romantic love, she had a good
laugh over the fact that her friend and lover
had made it through the forever of a first year.

Told me smells great but the next romantic
fragrance E. Taylor brings out should be called
Get real!—Taylor with her eight marriages
ya know yer sure yer fallin' in love
yer in La La Land ya pull out the antidote
splash it on yer wrists and temples spritz it down
yer blouse between yer breasts the backs of
yer knees and ya *get real* so ya go ahead
and have yer fun but keep yer heart on reserve
flowers are fine but I don't kowtow to any man
just cuz the romanticism I sometimes believe in
is takin' me over.

                      Get real! I said.
I sprayed on my impostor *Giorgio,* turned on the
ignition, popped a Hershey's chocolate kiss in
my mouth and the two of us drove, laughing
all the way through the rain to Red Lobster,
all the fish in the sea for us there, the waiters,
she said, cute enough to adopt, fumes of
scampi platters wafting our way.

All thought of *Eternity* gone now, although
I asked: don't we want our work, our sketches,
paintings, poems, books and quilts to go
beyond the century? For whatever beauty
and compassion, rhythm, motion, vision and
illumination, whatever exuberance they possess?

Asked me isn't that layin' it on a bit thick
it's enough to make me a vegetarian.
She ordered two dinner salads, cheesy biscuits,
flirted with the waiters, and said some of them looked
ripe for a fling with an older woman.
One of them responded, called her later,
but after some time with him, best lover she'd
ever had, she told me, she turned him loose.

Unseemly, she advised him, might work for
some women, but not me, she said, because
he distracted me too often from my work
I ended the romance even though I haven't
stopped flirting frolicking and gallivanting
from time to time. I now have turned
back to my work with new seriousness.

"Exuberance is beauty," I told her,
William Blake, *Proverbs from Hell.*

Told me she quit wearing any perfume at all and
was looking for friendship she could believe in,
build on, maybe not for an eternity, but for life.

She said her pheromones were probably dead anyway.

Girl Talk (subtexts)

Told me while searching for *the real*,
she found words covering the world with lies.

She said: in winter snow covers the earth
and I found I loved winter 'n the words
the lies even as I knew I would probably
love *the real* should I ever find it
gradually I let go warmed up I fell into silence

I planted flowers 'n herbs in small pots
carried food to the widow read to young children
gave art lessons now my words come less often
carry loads less weighty, she said, my work
my lies are *real* they are true they are mine.

I asked her, Even as my lines, my lies, are *real*?
Told her Plato had written somewhere about *play*.
The *plays*, on stage in the theater. Are they *real*?
One *plays* a musical instrument.

Told me and I agreed: love our work
it's play we're the lucky ones it's real.

Department Store Visit

I've missed the bus,
have a half hour to wait,
and enter the front doors bored
already by the hot, perfumed
smell of dye, shoppers and leather.
I remember when I sold lingerie
wore underwear.

I still wear underwear.
Here, I need everything and find
nothing but orange and fuchsia
pretty dresses that hang to the floor
from the hangers but hit my stork-like-
bird-thin legs midcalf.
And the horror of it when bikini
and bra sets, fits one size, never do.

Rack upon rack of pantsuitspeasant-
dresseswigssandalstrenchcoatshotpants
cutsiewootsienightiesaphrodisiacperfumes
mock me. And cost too much. And my
face in the mirror is pale and wan by now.
I think I've never looked so ill-suited
to any place in the world. Furious

I walk deliberately to the Women's Lounge and
pinch my cheeks, pat my hair, smooth my old
beige turtle neck sweater, my navy skirt and
smile, trying to look bright and twenty-five again.
The tired, resting grandmother here makes me
sure I do by comparison the teenage
cosmetic girl makes me stumble as I leave.

The bus will get me home in plenty of sun-
time and I'll put on enough to keep decent

for the neighbors and to please my love
and I'll slowly burn to a brown where
everything fits.

On Receiving a Postcard from St. Tropez

I put on my homemade bikini,
bright enough to cheer me,
made from material that looks
as though it came from a Chinese hock shop
(fuchsia, orange, yellow, blue, magenta and green)
and I head for a sunny space by the alley
behind the garage.

Reading the card now (which is French):
"On the beaches of St. Tropez, one can 'rub
elbows' with typical people like those
in the photograph."
Those being bronzed, nude, nineteen-year-olds
sunning themselves on yellow rocks.

I settle deeper into prairie sunshine
near the cinder and gravel and,
as much as I dare,
bare my bosom to the noon.

After covering myself with Swedish
Tanning Secret, I decide to read on:
"So far the trip to Mont Blanc—
highest mountain in Europe—
was the best thing we've done."

I peek under my bikini top at my breasts
growing whiter and flatter in the heat,
begin listening to the surf-like sounds
of crickets. Then, rolling over, elevate
my covered tush, my own Mont Blanc,
toss the postcard aside, and marinate
in a present geography.

Girl Talk (trail / horses)

Told her we're both so much in love
with making our marks on paper, leaving
a trail for ourselves, doubling back
when we become lost, but every way curious
about what's been pulling at us, not wanting
a return to the comfortable, predictable, bright
streets of the same old territories, rearing,
bucking, tossing those old riders off.

Wild horses, what we think we are,
I told her. Don't ever want to be broken.

Not horses, she said, pioneers or nomads
ramblers or rovers vagrants gypsies.

Archeologists, fugitives, I countered.
She crossed her eyes, tossed up her hands,
turned her face, returned to the postcards
for the artists and poets HIV/AIDS benefit.

Girl Talk (lingo)

Told her, yes, I'm in love with paper,
the wavelength of a rambling lingo,
keenings, foreshadowings, celebrations.

Reader and writer alike, as in mirrors,
find themselves, as one's face given back

on the surface of still water: lake or pond,
the work of our hands, a lover's eyes.

Girl Talk (buddha)

Early on she told me: talk about
be the thing you see your buddha

your shambhala nirvana zen
I've taken up calligraphy

a few words on a sketch are worth
an image or two 'n the italic does it

calms and slows the reader down
which I'm learning to do for myself

I don't turn to panic when I do
art work on an AIDS panel

I have this image of myself doing
exactly what I'm doing at any given moment

I guess that means I have presence
              or
that I'm present in the moment

Ommmmmmm, she chanted,

            Ommmmmmm

                  Ommmmmmmm

Girl Talk (the book / Job)

She made a fist, slammed it down on the table
barely missing her palette with blobs
of alizarin blue and cochineal red
for another HIV poster.

I was studying her collages and thought
how like people's lives. We seldom read
complete texts or sub-texts—even
our own, let alone another's. And there,
out of the turquoise blue ocean of her eyes,
her palette, her canvas, she asked me:

What if there were no Book of Job
the scabs the pestilence the lost fortunes
the eternal why whether or not
he should curse god 'n die this great
complainer like David who shook his fist
at God more than once like Jeremiah's
why me o lord I am but a youth 'n
cannot speak 'n Isaiah's how long
o lord how long—no wusses these
no eternal forgivers—an argument a wail
gets the blood flowing the adrenaline—

hide it then it festers it's the sharing of it
keeps us sane, she told me, sane
it somehow sometimes lets in light

'n how about Esther her wilyness her beauty
saving the Jews, she asked, or Judith
cutting off the head of the enemy's king

'n AIDS itself like an Old Testament plague.

6 On Holy Ground

Each separate being in the universe
   returns to the common source.
      Returning to the source is serenity.

Tao Te Ching (#16)

Poetry is not prayer,
   but it is not not prayer.

Carolyn Kizer, 1993

Night Summons
for JG

At midnight I'll wake you

        and take you to see the moonlight

the white blooming tree

Girl Talk (her art)
on a phrase from Anais Nin

She invited me to come over to her studio
while she sorted things out one at a time.

Told her you become the very thing you see, Friend,
and whatever you see: the only tree in the forest.

And you, yourself, *a tree with portable roots,*
linden or poplar, tree of paradise or locust,
orchard of apple trees, in bloom or in fruit,
you turn from tree to tree without getting lost.

Yes, she said, in my own world a palette
or canvas turpentine brushes paint
constructions texts collages still life
the studio chaotic a muddle a botch
a hodgepodge a mess 'n yet assembled
together a hybrid a wilderness savannah
verdant underbrush perennial seedlings.

Told me it's meditating develops her chi,
her energy, makes it possible. She elaborated,
I look around 'n say I can't be lost
I'm right here I focus I concentrate
forget the men and yes become
the thing I see landscape or collage
benefit announcement or quilt panel.

*

She studied her reflection, patted her hair,
frowned, then looked away from the mirror
into her canvas, a single tree, bending,
a willow this time, bending, bending.

Waiting for the Last Angel
for JG

They will never ask you
tho' the angels know the questions

Death in its cloud
dense as marble
small as a pebble
only one and imperfect

In the apple of Love
Death has polished
the seed of the fruit
implanted the worm

Even the limbs
of the cottonwood trees
are stripped
of their clattering leaves
and fly up
in a sky
empty
of light

Girl Talk (AIDS project / names)

Told her on that day, others read the names.

John

    Mark

        Marcia

            Gordon

Fred

    Annette

        David

            Angela

Told her I couldn't have read. Not even one name.
The music, Scottish laments and drones
on the dulcimer. Minor keys. No lyrics.

And continually, from 10 AM to 8 PM:
        The reading. The names.

Marie

    Ken

        Le Mar

            Manuel

Dennis

    Ruth

        Maria

            Darrell

On three consecutive days. The names. The music.

Chipper

    Todd

    Max

        Duane

Over and over. Beginning 1990, to the present day.

Sam

    Ron

        Jeff

            Ginny

Complete circles of names. Repeating each day.

And on quilt panels:

    "MILLIE   A SHINING STAR," all in caps.

And in bold: **"Morris Costa, our brave Warrior."**

    "Jim Magdanz . . . hugs from the heart."

        "We shall not forget."

    "Danny Will Be Remembered As A Man."

        "In Memory of Any Child"

    "Jeffrey, Now You're Our Guardian Angel"

        "Miguel Casanova, Rev. Calvin, Rev. Cliff. Rev. Grant"

This last one, signed:

        "Northern California United Church of Christ:
        our loved ones who walked into the Light."

"Take your shoes off, you're standing
    on Holy Ground."

Return
for JG

The west wind   tearing over and through
        rocky mountains and wrapped in clouds

arrives here on the plains wearing
        her thunder and lightning asking us

to befriend her by offering our tossing
        umbrellas   those old protections until

something in us longs to lay down
        our clothes as when we ran, children

through a new rain,   never asking
        to be cleansed.

Percival's Final Questions

Which earth is this, present or absent?
        Which crevasse is this, wider, narrower?

Which unuttered word, not my own,
        which past events, which darkness
will lift away forever?

What unrequited passion will shake
        its turbulent waters over my death bed?
And when did I ever fully live?

In which hour was I truly innocent?
        Which cup did I refuse?

Which embrace will prevail,
        will mark my life?

What will come from my hands
        as a deathless gift?

And in whose mind,
        as on a tabula rasa,
will my guilt rest?

In what guise do I wait,
        am I awaited?

Do I follow along?
        Am I to find the Host?
God's Gift? The Wine?

        What yellow bird sings?
                Why darker now
my arms, my smile?

        Who, and what,
                fills my heart with light,
and why?

The Tribe

We don't know from where and there's
little to know about it, but suddenly we find
ourselves, come together, tell stories.
Nomads, maybe. Eating, drinking,
on the move dancing, arguing, lighting up
huge fires. Not gypsies, exactly.

Sometimes we see someone leaving. Each man
by himself. Sometimes we have time to say
goodbye. Each woman alone. Sometimes not.
Some days, a child wanders away
from the quiet, the sometimes white water rivers.
We don't know how to reach them, these rovers.

As if they were still here, we laugh. Actors,
perhaps. Tell our side of old grievances, cry.
Some of us don't like to talk about it.
Some tell us they know where the others
have gone, but can't say what it's like there.
They've never visited—the ones who have left us.

If just once, one would come back.
If just once, one could talk about it,
coming back, tell us what's really there.
Or even what it was like in that first place
where we each began, in the ether,
before starting this journey together.

Each of us heading out alone.
Toward the same destination.
Other than in a dream.
Into that last white light.

Angel of the Hollow Hills
on two lines from Rilke, for JG

On my way to build mountains,
I summon the rain,
my apron full of stones.

You who sorrow, take my light.
It will show you the rock
where you can quarry your soul.

Abandoned on the mountains of the heart,
even there something can burst into flower.

Lullabye

Wrap your arms around your breast

Or make a cradle for your head

And dream as you turn down

The bed's dark street

Girl Talk (angels)

Told me she almost believes in angels.
God knows I need one, she said, because
there I was at the Gallery last Sunday
checkin' out the Holiday Show when an angel
came flyin' into me a tiny angel
red hair a gold halo pale yellow wings
wearin' a blue gown 'n holdin' a white dove.

Recalling the poem by Emily Dickinson
about angels living next door wherever we go,
I start to mention those lines but she went on
about her own angel looking like a bird
who must have been trying to fly away
without being at all helpful.

                              I wondered
out loud about how many run-ins with angels
she'd had in her life, in the Gallery, in her studio,
anywhere. She was working on an AIDS quilt
and ignored me, then blurted out how she'd bumped
a Gallery table with a small ceramic angel on it,
how the angel fell breaking off the wings. Now
she must buy it for twenty dollars.

Told me, she knew all along it was something
angelic trying to caution her so she took it
home, glued on the wings and soon she'd paint
an impression or two as reminder, a caution,
what with many of her friends in a world
of challenge or puzzlement over their health,
their kids, their parents, their check books,
their love life, just being hit, she told me,
square in the face with at least one catastrophe or
another, most of them without meditating on any of it
no angels, ceramic, bird-like, or spirit, unless you look.

She told me she has something tangible now
to remind her of how alone she is *not*.

As I left, I noticed how her face glowed,
how her studio filled with white light.

The Visitor

Some set a dining place for this,
    the uninvited guest,
        an empty place at the table,

set in remembrance.
    For generosity, compassion.

And there is that other visitor
    each of us expects,
        yet few expect to follow willingly.

The visitor even fewer of us invite.

    All will feel its presence
        as if a shooting star has dashed
            through the sky of an inner peace.

            Burst and flare of last light.

When It Is Over

The back arches
        the arms thrown overhead

then the words

"Your electric days
        are in my dying hands"

Hearing this
        the face lifts to the sun
                falls golden

It is meant for each of us
        life in such arms
                that when it is over
        we go in a cry of passion

Love: The Red, Red Rose?

Although resembling one, the female secret
when opening is not the pink rose, the flushed rose,
nor the deepening red rose.

And the metaphor, not the bridge we cross over
carrying our love to the blue lake of another's eyes.

La petite morte is only a little death
until the heart and lungs no longer cry out
in passion.

And death itself, not a passing away.

To where, we have eternally asked.
And who has returned to tell us?

The lover? Running down a hill,
arms held open for an embrace
as my father in the dream
my mother dreamed
after his sudden death
so many years ago?

Let It Happen

We start out in one direction

        one gesture at a time

                the mountain cannot find its way to us

As for the valley

        it will hold us long enough

                its shadow   the everlasting sleep

No Matter How Lost
for JG

Remember: what you call
        into the dark woods
                will come back to you.

In black marshy places
        are rivers of light
                and small white flowers
                      at your feet.

Girl Talk (every day / every night / walking out)

        into the east

                      into the sun

    which goes

                      everywhere

        standing at noon

                      in shadow

        my greeting

                      breathing it in

    breathing

                      into the dark

  into the west   the moon the stars

        the beyond: everywhere

greeting

          the nightly

                          sleep

greeting

          the long

                          sleep

Girl Talk (winning / losing)

We are walking along the river and
I tell her in middle age losing isn't
Everything. It questions whether
Whatever it was you won was really
Your idea, because of your plans,
Or simply an accident like slipping
On ice without breaking a bone or
Skinning your elbows and knees, then
Afterward standing straight up as if
In the first light after a blizzard, applause
Around you, leaves clattering in November.

Tells me some things can't be lost
Like that tree by the Platte the last
In the river valley to lose its yellow
Standing now just as it did
Breaking my heart ten years ago
With so much ice and wind
Not tearing or stripping its branches.

She continues, look around the curve
Beyond the river that two story
Stone house from a century ago
Almost a mansion in those days the house
We thought had been razed emerges
Through the stand of willow whose leaves
Fell over a long weekend as
Gradually as light leaves the prairie.

The view as clear as what we hope for,
I tell her. We continue our walking.

ALSO BY NANCY McCLEERY

Blown Roses, bradypress, 2001
Polar Lights, Transient Press, 1994
Staying the Winter, The Cummington Press, 1987
Postcards from London, The Red Press, 1985
Night Muse, Uintah Press, 1981

and libretti for muscial theatre pieces and songs
   by composer Robert Walters:

Green Tree of Lights, 1983
Rituals for Thanksgiving & Celebration, 1979
Nine Musical Pieces for piano, flute & soprano voice, 1978
A Gift From the River, 1976